HOLIDAY COLLECTION

D0927651

this book is for

_____

from

_____

on

_____

And the Word became flesh and dwelt
among us, and we have seen His glory,
glory as of the only Son from the Father,
full of grace and truth.

John 1:14

CHRISTMAS
AROUND the WORLD

By Brenda Trunkhill

Illustrations by Jeff Carnehl

CONCORDIA PUBLISHING HOUSE • SAINT LOUIS

Dear Parent(s),

Christmas is an exciting time for any child. Festive foods, colorful decorations, and memorable traditions make this a time of year like no other. Your child will be fascinated to hear how other children around the world celebrate throughout the holiday season in sometimes similar and sometimes very different ways.

But the story of this day is about another child . . . the Christ child . . . for He is why we celebrate Christmas. Because He cared so much for each of us, He left heaven to visit our sinful, broken world. The little baby in a manger would grow up to die on the cross and rise again, conquering sin and death, so all children every can someday join Him in heaven.

As you read this book, you may want to focus on one region at a time. Just as you wouldn't read an encyclopedia from cover to cover in one sitting, don't be discouraged if your child doesn't want to read more than a few pages at a time. Follow your child's lead, pointing out different facts, noting details in the illustrations and photographs, and asking questions to stimulate discussion.

As you "travel" around the world in this book, remember Jesus' travels and those of His apostles. Jesus made His home here on earth, becoming fully man, yet still fully God. He traveled throughout His homeland to teach about God's kingdom and the Gospel message of salvation through faith in Him. Then Jesus traveled back to heaven, where He is preparing a place for all of His children so they can live forever with Him.

Jesus came for *all* nations. Children around the world have different ways of celebrating the holiday, but we all celebrate the same thing . . . the birth of the Savior of the world. Jesus shines His light on all people, everywhere. We pray that your child is fascinated not only by what children in other countries do, but by what one special little Boy born in Bethlehem did 2,000 years ago.

In Christ,

The Editors

Latin America

(South America, Mexico, Spain, and others)

How do they celebrate the Christ Child's birth?

Most people in Latin American countries belong to the Catholic church and celebrating Jesus' birth is an important part of their faith.

On Christmas Eve (*Noche Buena*), Christians celebrate a midnight mass (*Misa de gallo*) or church service. This church service is named after the rooster because some people believe it was the first animal to announce Jesus' birth.

Many Catholic countries like Spain also celebrate the Feast of the Immaculate Conception on December 8. This celebration remembers when the angel Gabriel told Mary, "You will conceive in your womb and bear a son, and you shall call His name Jesus. He will be great and will be called the Son of the Most High" (Luke 1:31–31).

In Brazil and Mexico, people enjoy Christmas plays called *Los Pastores* (the shepherds). These plays tell the story of the angels' visit to the shepherds and of the visit of the Wise Men. Many Latin countries celebrate Christmas with *Las Posadas,* a nine-day celebration of the Christmas story. People act out Mary and Joseph's trip to Bethlehem, going house to house asking if the innkeepers have any room. Finally, one family lets everyone into their home for a party. A *piñata* filled with treats is broken.

In Venezuela, people go to church each morning in the weeks before Christmas. They may even roller skate to church! At bedtime on Christmas Eve, they may tie a string to their big toe and let the other end of the string hang out the window. The next morning, people walking by pull on the string hanging out the window to make sure everyone in the house is awake on Christmas morning.

Sometimes people shoot fireworks and ring church bells to celebrate.

How do they decorate?

Craft: Paper Lantern (farole)

In Mexico, they hang paper lanterns for decoration.

1. Glue the short edges of a piece of white construction paper together.

2. Glue strips of green and red paper diagonally around the lantern.

3. Add a paper strip to the top and hang.

The legend of the poinsettia began in Mexico. This legend tells that a boy wanted to bring a gift to baby Jesus. The boy was very poor and could give only a handful of green weeds. When he laid them on the manger, a beautiful star-shaped red flower appeared on each branch.

How do they say Merry Christmas?

Feliz Navidad *[faleece naveedead]* (Mexico)

Boas Festas (Brazil)

In many parts of this region, like Brazil, Santa is called *Papai Noel.* Many children, however, believe the gift-givers are the Three Kings or *el Niño Jesus,* the baby Jesus. On January 6 (Epiphany), Three Kings Day is celebrated. The night before, children set out their shoes and leave straw and carrots for the Wise Men's camels. The Kings are said to leave presents in the children's shoes.

What do they eat?

In Spain, an almond candy called *turron* is enjoyed at Christmas. Since the weather is warm, many families in Latin America have picnics or banquets outside. In Venezuela, many people enjoy *tostados* and coffee after church on Christmas Day.

What can we pray for?

Many people in these countries do not regularly attend worship services. Pray that more families in these countries would go to church and believe that Jesus is the Light of the world (John 1:5).

The Caribbean Islands

(Jamaica, Haiti, the Bahamas, Puerto Rico, and others)

How do they celebrate the Christ Child's birth?

Christmas is widely celebrated in island nations and people of all religions join in to worship Jesus, who came to earth to save mankind from sin. Many of the traditions from other countries, such as Christmas music, gift-giving, special foods, and parades have been incorporated into island celebrations.

For example, in Jamaica, the Bahamas, and Puerto Rico, *Jonkonnu,* a parade, takes place the day after Christmas and on New Year's Day. In the evening, people watch or participate in a parade with dancing, stiltwalkers, and calypso music, and vibrant costumes. In other countries, the parade is called the *Masquerade* after the elaborate masks and costumes people wear. Costumes for the parade are often created in secret. People may spend time all year making costumes with feathers, fabrics, wood, and tissue.

Music is a very popular part of Caribbean Christmas celebrations. Carols and hymns from other countries are adapted to be played with island instruments such as guitar, flutes, maracas, tambourines, and steel drums. In Trinidad and Tobago, people celebrate Jesus' birth with parang music. Musicians go from house to house playing instruments and singing about the angel Gabriel's announcement to Mary and about the birth of Christ.

How do they decorate?

People decorate with Christmas trees and pine boughs. They hang bright ornaments on their trees and place Nativity scenes under the trees.

Craft: Seashell Ornament

1. Paint a shell with gold paint or cover it with clear nail polish or shellac.

2. Glue on a loop of gold ribbon for hanging. Glue on a small flower or bow to cover the loop.

3. Or use acrylic paint on a sand dollar; after it is dry, spray on an acrylic finish, and string gold ribbon to hang.

In Jamaica, Christmas markets are colorfully decorated with streamers, large paper bells, and balloons of all sizes, shapes, and colors. Many islanders thoroughly clean their house before Christmas and some people repaint inside and out and add new curtains and furniture.

How do they say Merry Christmas?
Merry Christmas!

Many children in this tropical region believe Santa Claus comes from under the sea, not the North Pole. Some countries like Haiti have a French influence, so they call Santa Claus *Papa Noël.*

What do they eat?

Special food is a big part of Caribbean Christmas celebrations. Roast pork, ham, and goat are common. In places like Jamaica, people of all ages enjoy imported fruit and local coffee; adults may consume a drink made from sorrel. In countries such as Puerto Rico, they enjoy cornmeal pasties (filled with meat, olives, capers, and raisins) called *pastelles.*

In many island countries, it is a Christmas tradition to make a black rum cake. Before we could mail packages so quickly, people would make these cakes two months before Christmas and soak them in rum so they wouldn't spoil. They would ship the cakes as presents to their loved ones across the ocean in plenty of time for them to arrive before December 25.

What can we pray for?

Although many people in this region say they are Christian, only about one-third of them go to church. Pray that parents provide a loving, stable home for their children and that they teach their children that Jesus, the Savior of the world, was born on Christmas.

Africa

(Nigeria, Ethiopia, Ghana, Egypt, South Africa, and more)

How do they celebrate the Christ Child's birth?

Christianity in Africa dates back to the first century AD in Egypt, when St. Mark brought the Gospel message to the people there. And we know from the Bible that Joseph, Mary, and baby Jesus lived in Egypt to hide from wicked King Herod, who wanted to kill the newborn King Jesus.

Today, there are an estimated 350 million Christians living in Africa, mostly in the southern countries. Because religion is a major part of everyday life, Christians in Africa love to teach about and learn about Jesus. And worshiping Him is the emphasis of Christmas celebrations.

At Christmas, Christians in African countries share simple gifts like baked goods and new clothes. Wearing new clothing to church on Christmas is a common tradition. On Christmas Eve, many people in Africa celebrate by singing carols, going to church, sharing a special offering, and watching nativity plays. In Liberia, people may set off fireworks. In Nigeria, children in costumes hold sparklers as they go from house to house acting out the nativity story and collecting money for church.

3 1833 05803 3835

How do they decorate?

In Liberia and many other African countries, palm trees are decorated with bells or other ornaments. In Africa, palm trees are symbols of peace. Oftentimes guava, mango, and cashew trees are decorated too! Designs are cut into crepe paper and it is used as garland.

Christians in African countries also decorate with lights, candles, colored lamps, and manger scenes.

How do they say Merry Christmas?

Melkm Ganna (Ethiopia) *Wishing you a happy Christmas*

Afishapa (Ghana) *Merry Christmas and happy New Year*

Eku Odun Ebi Jesu (Nigeria)

happy celebration or birth of Jesus Christ

Heri ya Christmas [hay-ree yah krees-mahs] Swahili

Geseënde Kersfees (South Africa) Afrikaans

Children in Africa most often call Santa "Santa Claus" or "Father Christmas." But in instead of leaving milk and cookies, in Ethiopia children leave him some of their delicious coffee. And in Egypt, Santa may be seen riding a camel.

What do they eat?

Because of the warm weather, many Africans eat an outdoor dinner. Rice and beef are common, and so are stews like okra soup, also porridge, and yam paste (*fufu*), which is dipped in very peppery soup.

In Ethiopia they use a pancake-like bread (*injera*) as a spoon to eat *doro wat* (a spicy chicken stew).

At Christmas Eve services in Egypt, people are given a special bread called *Qurban,* which is decorated with a cross surrounded by twelve dots that represent the twelve apostles.

What can we pray for?

Pray that these countries can recover from problems caused by war, drought, and famine.
Pray that God would bless the efforts of church workers
who serve God in these countries.

The British Isles

(England, Ireland, Scotland, and Wales)

How do they celebrate the Christ Child's birth?

Because this is a Christian region, Christ's birth has been celebrated here for hundreds and hundreds of years, and many of the churches where people go for Christmas worship were built centuries ago.

Many of the traditions we know began in this region of the world. For example, caroling began in England more than 500 years ago as a way that Christians could share their faith. Today, groups of carolers dance around in a circle or travel from house to house, singing songs of joy and faith in Jesus. In Wales, someone often plays a harp to accompany the singers.

Ireland has been a Christian country for about 1500 years, and Christmas is the most important celebration of the year. Traditionally, people celebrate the twelve days of Christmas (the birth of Christ to Epiphany). To prepare, they clean their houses and even whitewash the outside walls as a way to honor the coming Christ Child.

In Scotland, Christmas celebrations were considered to be be pagan (non-Christian) and were illegal until about 50 years ago. Since then, Christian Christmas celebrations have become much like they are elsewhere in the United Kingdom. Scotland's traditional winter festival is *Hogmanay,* which takes place on New Year's Day. People celebrate with bonfires and fireworks.

On December 26, people in this region of the world observe Boxing Day, when offering boxes at church are opened and money is given to poor.

How do they decorate?

People in Ireland place a lighted candle in a window to symbolize hospitality to the Holy Family.

People in the British Isles hang greenery like holly and ivy to symbolize the eternal life we have through faith in Jesus Christ.

To remind them of a crackling fire, people in England leave a "cracker" by each plate at the dinner table on Christmas. When it's pulled open, a surprise, such as a small toy or candy or a riddle, pops out.

Make a Christmas "cracker":

1. Wrap paper around a toilet paper roll, with some extra hanging over each end.

2. Tie a piece of ribbon to close one end. Fill the roll with candy and confetti. Then tie the other end with ribbon.

How do they say Merry Christmas?
Happy Christmas!

Many children put out stockings for Father Christmas to fill. Legend says that Father Christmas once dropped a few gold coins as he was coming down the chimney. The family had hung their socks by the fire to dry, so the coins landed inside! Now on Christmas Eve, many children hang stockings, hoping to find them filled with gifts.

What do they eat?

In England, people wish others, "Good health!" and drink *wassail* (hot punch) together. They usually do this after caroling. Christmas dinner used to be a roasted boar's head, but today it is most often a turkey dinner with a plum pudding dessert.

In Scotland, people eat *sowans,* a dish made from oats.

In Ireland, people have a festive Christmas dinner that may include spiced beef and a seed cake for each person. Some families in Ireland have twelve different foods at dinner to symbolize the twelve days of Christmas.

What can we pray for?

Most people in England say they are Christians, but few go to church. We can pray that people in the United Kingdom would read the Bible and learn that we have the hope of living in heaven with Jesus one day.

Europe

(France, Scandinavian countries, Germany)

How do they celebrate the Christ Child's birth?

After Jesus' ascension, His apostles traveled to many lands to teach about Him and to baptize people in His name. The countries of Europe were among the first Christian countries in history. Since 200 or 300 AD, people in Europe have worshiped Jesus and celebrated His birth.

France is the home of many beautiful churches where Christian families celebrate Jesus' birth at midnight mass with special services and songs. Christmas in France is called *Noël*, which comes from the phrase *les bonnes nouvelles,* meaning "the good news."

Christmas traditions in German homes include an Advent wreath and Advent calendar. Each day in December, children open a window in their Advent calendar to find a treat or Bible verse. And one candle on an Advent wreath is lit each week in the month. Many people enjoy shopping at a *Christkindlemarkt* (Christ Child market) in German cities and villages.

In Scandinavian countries like Finland and Sweden, the Christmas celebration begins with St. Lucia Day, December 13. On this day, the oldest daughter serves her family cakes and candy. She wears a crown or wreath of candles on her head and wears a white gown. Saint Lucia was martyred for her faith.

14

How do they decorate?

The custom of the Christmas tree, or *tannenbaum*, began in Germany in the 1500s. In some German homes, the last ornament put on the tree is a glass pickle, hidden in the branches. The first child to find the ornament on Christmas morning receives an extra present.

In Finland, Christmas trees are decorated with apples, candies, flags, and tinsel. An arrangement of grain, nuts, and seeds is tied on a pole for birds. Straw may be hung from the ceiling as a mobile (*himmeli*).

Homes in Sweden are decorated with red flowers such as poinsettia and amaryllis.

Elaborately decorated *sapins de Noël* (Christmas trees) and *crèches* are the main decorations in French homes and public places.

How do they say Merry Christmas?

Joyeux Noël *[zhwah-yehr no-ehl]* (France)

Hyvää Joulua! (Finland)

Froehliche Weihnachten *[fore-lich-eh vahy-nach-ten]* (Germany)

God Jul ... och ett Gott Nytt Ar! (Sweden)

In France, *Pere Noël* hangs sweets, fruits, nuts, and toys on the tree. Instead of stockings, children may leave their shoes by the fireplace.

Children in Germany set out their shoes the night before St. Nicholas Day, December 6. *Weihnachtsmann* (Christmas Man) or the *Christkind* (a messenger or angel of the Christ Child) places gifts in them.

In Finland, *Joulupukki* brings gifts and some people tell stories about a Yule goat that visits homes.

In Sweden, *Tomte* hands out gifts to children and says little rhymes.

What do they eat?

In France, *le Réveillon* is a supper eaten after midnight mass (church service) on Christmas Eve. This supper symbolizes the awakening to Christ's birth. A traditional French dessert is log-shaped cake called *la bûche de Noël*.

In Finland, gingerbread hearts and stars are often part of a Christmas meal. Germans also make gingerbread cookies (*pfefferkuchen*) and eat *stollen* (a dried fruit and nut bread or coffeecake).

A rice pudding called *risgryngrot* is served in Sweden at Christmas meals. One almond is baked in this pudding. The person who receives the almond gets to make a wish.

What can we pray for?

Only one in four Germans regularly goes to church. In Finland, only four percent of the membership attends church regularly. Pray that the Holy Spirit moves people in this region go to church to hear God's Word of salvation.

Russia

How do they celebrate the Christ Child's birth?

According to tradition, the people in this region learned about Jesus when the Apostle Andrew came here on his missionary journeys. For a time, though, the people did not celebrate Christmas because the government banned religious celebrations. This changed in 1992 and now Jesus' birth is openly celebrated.

In Russia, Christmas is celebrated on January 7, which corresponds to December 25 on their calendar (Julian Calendar). On Christmas Eve, when the first star in the evening sky appears, families gather around the table to remember Jesus' birth with "The Holy Supper." A white tablecloth reminds the family of the baby's swaddling cloths. Hay is used as a decoration to remind the family of the humble animal stall where Jesus was born. A tall white candle in the center of the table reminds that Jesus is the "Light of the World." After the meal, families open presents and go to church.

But not all people in this region celebrate Christmas. Russia has beautiful, old cathedrals, but many are empty because fewer than five percent of the people here attend church regularly. In Kazakhstan, sixty percent of the people are Muslim. In Kyrgystan, eighty percent of the people are Muslim.

How do they decorate?

People in Russia decorate with trees and ornaments. *Yolka* (Christmas trees) may be decorated with handmade ornaments and fruit. Have you seen Russian nesting dolls? They come in different sizes, so the smaller ones fit inside the larger ones. Some look like *Babushka* or like *matryoshka* (Snow Maiden).

How do they say Merry Christmas?
S Roždestvom Khristovym

In Russia, Santa is often called Grandfather Frost (*Dedushka Moroz*). But it is *Babushka* (grandmother) who brings gifts. A story is told that the wise men visited her home on their way to see Jesus, but she stayed behind to clean. Ever since then, Babushka has been trying to find the Christ Child.

What do they eat?

Kutya is a special porridge that symbolizes hope, happiness and success.

On January 6 many people in Russia enjoy a 12-course supper to remember the 12 apostles. The meal includes *borsch* (beet soup). And they serve a large round loaf of bread (*pagach*) because Jesus is the Bread of Life.

What can we pray for?

We can pray that the people in Russia and countries nearby know Jesus is our Savior and find hope and comfort that He came to save all people everywhere.

Asia

(China, India, Vietnam, Japan, Korea, and others)

How do they celebrate the Christ Child's birth?

People in Asia enjoy the holiday but because most people are not Christian, few celebrate the birth of Christ. Christmas is a public holiday only in Hong Kong and Macau; if you lived in China, you would go to school on Christmas!

Half of Vietnamese people are Buddhists and 83 percent of the people in Myanmar worship Buddha. Most people in Asia also worship their ancestors and spirits. But Christianity is growing throughout all of Asia, and especially in China, where one percent are Christian—which is ten million baptized people!

For those people in China and Vietnam who are Christian, some will attend a midnight mass (church service). On Christmas Day, the Japanese like to exchange presents and spend the day helping the sick and poor.

In China, Christmas happens at the same time as their Spring Festival, when families honor their ancestors. During this festival, families enjoy a meal together, open presents, and set off firecrackers.

Although most of the people in India are Hindus and Muslims, not Christians, Christmas Day (*Bada Din* or "Big Day") is a national holiday and Christians who live there celebrate with long church services. For instance, in the state of Goa, a midnight mass could last three hours!

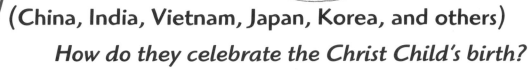

How do they decorate?

Christmas trees (trees of light) are decorated with colored lanterns, paper chains, paper flowers, and many lights. In Japan, gold paper fans, wind chimes, and origami swans or cranes are also added to trees. In cities, stores put up elaborate decorations.

In India, families decorate banana or mango trees inside their homes and cover ceilings corner to corner with streamers, fancy garlands, and balloons. Churches often decorate with poinsettias. In southern India, small oil-burning clay lamps are placed on the flat rooftops and walls of their homes.

How do they say Merry Christmas?

Meri Kurisumasu (Japan)

Kung His Hsin Nien bing Chu Shen Tan! (China—Cantonese)

Sheng Dan Kuai Le [*Shung Dahn Kwai Luh*] (China—Mandarin)

Chung Mung Giang Sinh! [*Chook mung jeeyahng sing*] (Vietnam)

Bade Din ki Mubarak (India)

In China, it is *Dun Che Lao Ren* (Christmas old man), not the Santa Claus many of us are familiar with, who fills muslin stockings with gifts.

In Japan, *Santa Kurohsu* or the priest *Hoteiosho* has eyes in the back of his head to see if children are good.

Vietnamese children leave shoes outside on Christmas Eve so Santa can fill them with presents.

What do they eat?

In Vietnam, people might eat chicken soup for Christmas. Wealthy people may have Christmas pudding.

In Japan, they also eat chicken, but it is usually a bucket of Kentucky Fried Chicken! For dessert, a Christmas cake topped with white frosting and strawberries is often served.

What can we pray for?

Pray that God's Word continues to spread freely throughout this region. And pray that Christian missionaries are welcomed by people in Asia.

The Middle East

(Turkey, Iraq, Lebanon, Pakistan, Syria, and others)

How do they celebrate the Christ Child's birth?

Most people in this part of the world are Muslim, not Christian and do not observe Jesus' birth.

In Saudi Arabia, it is against the law to celebrate Christmas! It really is a "silent night" because there are no Christian churches there, only Muslim mosques. If you are caught with a Christmas tree or a Bible, they will be taken away and you may be punished.

But this is not true for all countries in this region of the world. Lebanon openly celebrates Christmas as an official holiday. On Christmas Eve, families there attend a midnight mass (church service). And Christians in Pakistan celebrate *Bara Din*, which means "big day," with a procession to church. After the late night service on Christmas Eve, people may shoot off fireworks.

In Iraq, Christians usually have a bonfire at home, and at church they carry a figure of Jesus into church on a red cushion and pass a "touch of peace" throughout the congregation.

Christmas in Syria is also celebrated with a bonfire. On Christmas Eve, the youngest member of the family lights the bonfire with a candle. Then they read the story of Jesus' birth and sing psalms. Very early on Christmas morning, Christians go to church where there is another bonfire. As the fire burns, people sing ancient hymns and a figure of the Christ Child is carried around the building. Syria is the home of Damascus, where the Apostle Paul preached the Gospel.

How do they decorate?

Christmas decorations in Lebanon are white. To the Lebanese, white is the color of peace. Because of all the fighting in their land, the people there hope for peace.

Several weeks before Christmas, Lebanese people plant wheat, lentils, and bean seeds in small dishes with cotton balls. By Christmas, the seeds have sprouted and grown about six inches. The sprouts are used to

decorate homes and manger scenes. Nativity figures are often made from brown paper.

Christian homes in Pakistan are decorated with manger scenes, lights, Christmas trees, and a big star on the rooftops.

Craft:

Make your own white dove ornament. Simply trace the outline of a dove on white cardstock. Cut out the dove, punch a hole near the top, and hang it with gold ribbon.

How do they say Merry Christmas?

Meelad majeed *(Birth Glorious)* (Lebanese)

I'D Miilad Said Oua Sana Saida (Arabic)

The legend of Santa Claus began from a story about Nicholas, a pastor who lived in Myra, which is present day Turkey. Nicholas is said to have given a poor family a bag of gold coins.

In Lebanon, *Papa Noel* drops off gifts at the Christmas Eve service or visits with children in their homes. Presents are usually candy and clothes.

In Afghanistan *Baba Chaghaloo* brings gifts.

Children in Syria receive gifts on Epiphany from a camel. According to legend, this is the smallest camel that traveled with the Magi when they sought the new born King to worship Him.

What do they eat?

On Christmas Day in Lebanon, people visit friends in the morning and munch on almonds and drink coffee. Then they gather with their whole family (usually at the grandparents' home) and eat lunch together. Traditional foods at that lunch are chicken, rice, a soup called *sheesh barak*, *kubedeh* (finely ground beef or lamb), and *tabbouleh* (bulgur, mint, parsely, and tomato salad), and pastries made with honey and nuts (*baklava*).

What can we pray for?

Pray for the safety of the people in the Middle East. Also pray for hope and safety for soldiers in Iraq and for all military chaplains to know how best to deliver the Good News of comfort and joy.

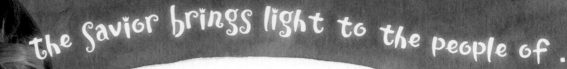
The Mediterranean

(Greece and Italy)

How do they celebrate the Christ Child's birth?

The people in Greece and Italy were some of the first Gentiles (people who weren't Jews) to believe in Jesus as Savior. In Greece, 98 percent are Greek Orthodox Christians and in Italy, about 90 percent are Roman Catholic. Christmas celebrations in this region of the world begin on December 6 (St. Nicholas Day) and end a month later on Epiphany as Christians celebrate the birth of our Savior.

In Italy, the word used for Christmas is *natale*, which means "birth." In the days just before Christmas Day, people set up elaborate nativity scenes. Then on Christmas Eve, the figure of baby Jesus is added to the scenes. At some places in the Alps, hundreds of skiers carry burning torches during a parade down the mountains! In the Vatican City, people from all over the world go to a midnight mass at St. Peter's Square.

In Greece, the main religious holiday is Easter, but they also celebrate our Savior's birth with festivals and traditions. On Christmas Eve, children go from house to house singing *kalandas* (carols). On Christmas Day, people attend a special worship service. The season winds down with the *Theophania*, or "Blessing of the Waters," which is celebrated on Epiphany to remember Jesus' Baptism. A priest blesses a cross and throws it into the Mediterranean Sea. The first young man to dive into the cold waters and bring back the cross is believed to have good luck in the next year. The priest also blesses the boats and ships in the harbor.

How do they decorate?

It is said that the idea of a Nativity scene came from St. Francis of Assisi in Italy almost 800 years ago. Today beautiful crèche displays are found in most churches and many homes. Crèche displays (*presepi*) not only show the stable, but often include an entire village or part of town, with people, trees, lakes, and rivers.

In Greece, towns are lavishly decorated with lights and trees, and almost every home decorates for St. Basil's Day, January 1. A sprig of basil wrapped around a wooden cross is hung from a wire above a bowl of water to keep the basil fresh. Every day, the basil is dipped in water and sprinkled around the house.

How do they say Merry Christmas?
Buon Natale! (Italy)
Kala Christouyenna (Greece)

Some children in Italy believe *babo natale* (Father Christmas) brings presents on Christmas. But most children in Italy find their gifts on Epiphany, January 6. The night before, children leave their shoes out in hopes that *La Befana,* an old woman who travels throughout Italy on a broom, will leave toys and candy inside them.

In Greece, St. Nicholas is the patron saint of sailors. They believe his beard drips with water because he rescues sailors from the rough waves. It is St. Basil who brings gifts. On New Year's Day he travels in a boat to get to children's homes!

What do they eat?

In Italy, a Christmas Eve feast includes at least seven different kinds of seafood (like cod, eel, squid, clams, and conch). Dessert may be a cake filled with candied fruit (*panettone*) or gingerbread (*panforte*). Christmas sweets almost always are made with nuts and honey.

In Greece, a Christmas pig is served. Most families also serve a "Christ bread" (*Christopsomo*) that is decorated to show what the father does for a living. The bread is served with honey, dried fruits, and nuts. Traditional Christmas cookies are *melomakarona*, which are flavored with cinnamon and cloves. On Saint Basil's Day, the family eats a sponge cake (*vasilopeta*). It is said that whoever finds a coin baked into their piece will have good luck in the New Year.

What can we pray for?

Pray that people in these areas, where Paul traveled on his missionary journeys, would again hear the Good News about Jesus.

Australia

How do they celebrate the Christ Child's birth?

Australia's native people—the Aborigines—are not Christian and do not celebrate Christmas. But about two-thirds of the non-native people who live in Australia are Christian and there is a growing population of Muslims and Buddhists. Even if they're not Christian, though, people throughout the continent enjoy celebrating Christmas as a secular holiday.

Christmas in Australia falls during summer vacation from school! Many families go camping or stay at the beach. Bondi Beach near Sydney is a popular vacation spot.

On Christmas Eve, many people attend or listen on the radio to a "Carols by Candlelight" concert in Melbourne.

Christian families celebrate Christmas together, often attending a late night church service on Christmas Eve and again early Christmas morning.

The day after Christmas, Boxing Day, is celebrated by giving money (collected in boxes) to the needy. People visiting or living along the coast near Sydney watch yacht races held that day.

There is actually a small territory in the Indian Ocean near Australia called Christmas Island, because that's the day explorers found it hundreds of years ago.

How do they decorate?

Since it's summer in Australia, they simply decorate with fresh flowers. Other Christmas decorations in Australia are similar to those seen in the United States, such as lights, trees, and wreaths.

Craft: Christmas Stocking

1. Cut a stocking shape from paper or felt, and carefully sew around the edges.

2. Decorate the front of the stocking by gluing on sequins, beads, braid or trim, or felt shapes (like stars and holly leaves).

3. Hang the stocking, or fill it with inexpensive gifts and candy and give it to someone special.

How do they say Merry Christmas?
Merry Christmas!

Instead of leaving out milk and cookies, children in Australia leave out cold lemonade for Santa Claus. Have you ever seen a surfing or waterskiing Santa? In some towns, Santa arrives at the beach in a boat.

What do they eat?

Christmas dinner is often eaten as a picnic on the beach. People often eat seafood on Christmas, but that day's dinner might also be turkey or ham. Special cakes called *lamingtons* are a Christmas treat in Australia. Another special dessert is plum pudding.

What can we pray for?

We can pray that all people in Australia recognize the need to go to church and hear God's Word, which is a lamp to our feet and a light to our path (Psalm 119:105).

The Holy Land

(Palestine, Israel)

How do they celebrate the Christ Child's birth?

Although Jesus Christ lived and died in this region of the world, most people who live here today are Jewish or Muslim. Palestine, where Bethlehem is located, is not a Christian country. Only 2.1 percent of the people call themselves Christian. People go to work on Christmas and do not celebrate the Savior's birth.

Many Christians here are afraid for their safety. But they still honor Jesus by celebrating His birth! People in Bethlehem have made a silver star with 14 points on the floor at the spot they think was the cave where He was born. Hundreds of years ago a church was built around the spot. It is called the Church of the Nativity. A public gathering area called Manger Square is directly outside the church.

On Christmas Eve a parade or procession quietly enters the doors to the Church of the Nativity. And Christians from other countries sometimes visit Bethlehem to celebrate the Savior's birth. There are three worship services at the Church of the Nativity on Christmas Eve: Protestant/Catholic, Greek Orthodox, and Armenian.

How do they decorate?

At Christmastime, flags and decorations add color to Manger Square. A star is set up on a pole there. People walk down steps to see the cave where it is believed Jesus was born. In the cave is a shiny silver star and fifteen silver lamps.

Craft: Shining Silver Star

Trace or draw a star onto poster board or corrugated board. Cover it completely with the shiny side of aluminum foil. With an adult's help, poke a hole in the star. Then thread yarn or string through the hole and hang the star in a window.

How do they say Merry Christmas?

I'D Miilad Said ous Sana Saida (Arabic)

Shenoraavor Nor Dari yev Pari Gaghand (Armenian)

Mo'adim Lesimkha (Hebrew)

What do they eat?

During Christmas time, many people in Israel celebrate Hanukah, a Jewish holiday also known as the Festival of Lights. Jelly-filled doughnuts (*sufganiyot*) are part of that celebration. People also eat potato pancakes (*latkas*) and dairy products, especially cheese.

What can we pray for?

Pray that people in Palestine realize what happened long ago that holy night, in their own land: Jesus, their Savior was born! We can also pray that the leaders of the region stop hurting one another and let Christians openly worship Jesus.

United States and Canada

How do they celebrate the Christ Child's birth?

This region in the world was settled by Christians and religion is an important part of everyday life. Throughout the country, Christmas is the most popular holiday of the year as people remember that Jesus was born as the Savior of the world.

In the weeks before Christmas, Americans buy and wrap presents to give to family and friends. Many also send greeting cards to loved ones and go caroling. People may attend special Christmas concerts, plays, parties, or parades. Homes and businesses may have Christmas decorations, such as trees, wreaths, manger scenes, and lights. Some communities have elaborate Christmas displays set up in parks that people drive by to look at.

Advent is a time of preparation for Christ's birth. Many Christians attend Advent services held at church during the middle of the week and have Advent calendars or wreaths in their homes.

On Christmas Eve or Christmas morning, families attend a church service and exchange gifts. Children are often involved in a Christmas service, and choirs and special music are usually a part of the worship services throughout Advent and Christmas.

People in the South often shoot off fireworks to celebrate Christmas Eve. And people in Alaska may carry a large star on a pole from door to door as they sing carols.

How do they decorate?

Most places are filled with twinkling lights and colorful decorations. Many people decorate their houses and yards and have a Christmas tree inside. Nativity scenes are often seen at churches. And Advent wreaths are used in homes and in churches too.

Craft:
Advent Wreath

Using a green foam wreath ring, have an adult cut four evenly-spaced holes to hold candles. Poke in or glue on enough evergreens (such as fir, holly, or ivy) or silk greencry to cover the wreath. You may also add small pinecones, red berries, poinsettias, or ribbons.

How do they say Merry Christmas?
Merry Christmas!

More and more people use the words, "Happy Holidays!" so they don't hurt anyone's feelings if they're not Christian and don't celebrate Christmas.

Santa Claus comes down the chimney on Christmas Eve, leaving presents under the tree and in stockings hung by the fireplace.

What do they eat?

Christmas dinner usually includes turkey, duck, goose, or ham. There may also be candy canes, fruitcakes, and eggnog at Christmas parties. Baking and sharing Christmas cookies is a popular activity in all parts of the United States.

What can we pray for?

Say a prayer of thanks that Jesus promises to be with us and gives us the Holy Spirit to help us. Also thank God that we live in a Christian nation where we can worship our Savior without fear.

1 Sav-ior of the na-tions, come, Vir-gin's Son, make
2 Not by hu-man flesh and blood, By the Spir-it
3 Here a maid was found with child, Yet re-mained a
4 Then stepped forth the Lord of all From His pure and

here Your home! Mar-vel now, O heav'n and earth,
of our God, Was the Word of God made flesh—
vir-gin mild. In her womb this truth was shown:
king-ly hall; God of God, yet ful-ly man,

That the Lord chose such a birth.
Wom-an's off-spring, pure and fresh.
God was there up-on His throne.
His he-ro-ic course be-gan.

5 God the Father was His source,
Back to God He ran His course.
Into hell His road went down,
Back then to His throne and crown.

6 For You are the Father's Son
Who in flesh the vict'ry won.
By Your mighty pow'r make whole
All our ills of flesh and soul.

7 From the manger newborn light
Shines in glory through the night.
Darkness there no more resides;
In this light faith now abides.

8 Glory to the Father sing,
Glory to the Son, our king,
Glory to the Spirit be
Now and through eternity.

PHOTOGRAPHY and ART CREDITS

Front Cover
Title banner © Russell Tate/iStockphoto.com
Globe © Edward Grajeda/iStockphoto.com
Children, clockwise:
© Jacom Stephens/iStockphoto.com
© Roger McClean/iStockphoto.com
© Christian Chris/iStockphoto.com
© Terrie L. Zeller, 2009/Shutterstock, Inc.
© Wojciech Gajda/iStockphoto.com
© Scrg Zasatavkin/Shutterstock, Inc.
© iStockphoto.com
© Rafik El Raheb/iStockphoto.com
© Tari Faris/iStockphoto.com
© Rosemarie Gearhart/iStockphoto.com
© Noam Armonn/iStockphoto.com
© Rosemarie Gearhart/iStockphoto.com

Back Cover
Girl © Tina Lorien/ iStockphoto.com
Boy © Vikram Raghuvanshi/ iStockphoto.com

Page 3
Title banner © Russell Tate/iStockphoto.com
Globe © Edward Grajeda/iStockphoto.com
Children, top to bottom:
© Danish Khan/iStockphoto.com
© iStockphoto.com
© Mags Ascough/Shutterstock, Inc.

Page 4
Girl with globe © Ramona Heim/Shutterstock, Inc.

Page 5
Globe ornament © South 12th Photography/Shutterstock, Inc.

Pages 6–28
World map © Jayesh Bhagat/iStockphoto.com

Pages 6 & 7
Boy top left © Jacom Stephens/iStockphoto.com
Girl with piñata © Jesus Jauregui/iStockphoto.com
Argentinian church © Shutterstock, Inc.
Fireworks © iStockphoto.com
Nativity © Andres Balcazar/iStockphoto.com
Poinsettia © Shutterstock, Inc.
Family picnic © iStockphoto.com
Spanish turron © iStockphoto.com
Mexican Epiphany bread © Andres Balcazar/iStockphoto.com

Pages 8 & 9
Boy top left © Roger McClean/iStockphoto.com
Steel drum player © Alan Crawford/iStockphoto.com
Costumed woman © Jan Kranendonk/Shutterstock, Inc.
Two girls © Benjamin Howell/iStockphoto.com
Girl close up © Alex Gomez/iStockphoto.com
Nativity © Carmen Martinez Banus/iStockphoto.com
Seashell ornament © Jim Pruitt/iStockphoto.com
Cake © iStockphoto.com
Coconut stand © Brian Murphy/iStockphoto.com
Jamaican church © Raido Väljamaa/iStockphoto.com

Pages 10 & 11
Boy top left © Cristian Chris/iStockphoto.com
Girl in yellow © Peeter Viisimaa/iStockphoto.com
Ethiopian church © Robert Bremec/iStockphoto.com
Boy, bottom © iStockphoto.com
Nativity © Keith Muratori/Shutterstock, Inc.
Okra stew © Monkey Business Images/Shutterstock, Inc.
Cut yam © iStockphoto.com

Pages 12 & 13
Girl top left © Terrie L. Zeller/Shutterstock, Inc.
Scottish parade © Igor Vorobyov/iStockphoto.com
Girl in red © Eileen Hart/iStockphoto.com
Baby © Karen Squires/iStockphoto.com
Nativity © Mike Sonnenberg/iStockphoto.com
Holly & ivy © Gillian Mowbray/Shutterstock, Inc.
Stockings © Nikolay Okhitin/Shutterstock, Inc.
Wassail © Ingrid Balabanova/Shutterstock, Inc.
Christmas pudding © Donna Poole/iStockphoto.com

Pages 14 & 15
Girl top left © Wojciech Gajda/iStockphoto.com
Boy in blue © Roman Kobzarev/iStockphoto.com
Advent wreath © Mike Sonnenberg/iStockphoto.com
Boy with garland © Michaela Stejskalova/Shutterstock, Inc.
Nativity © iStockphoto.com
Straw ornament © Concettina D'Agnese/Shutterstock, Inc.
Straw Yule goat © Martin Carlsson/iStockphoto.com
Swedish cookies © iStockphoto.com

PHOTOGRAPHY and ART CREDITS